ISLAND

a memoir

ELAINE PACE

Illustrations by Ann Howes

Elaine Pace

www.memories101.us

Published by 1stWorld Publishing
1100 North 4th St. Suite 131, Fairfield, Iowa 52556
tel: 641-209-5000 • fax: 641-209-3001
web: www.1stworldpublishing.com

First Edition

LCCN: 2005928028
SoftCover ISBN: 1-59540-947-5
eBook ISBN: 1-59540-946-7

Book interior and cover design by Liz Howard

ABOUT THE AUTHOR

Elaine Pace is a Massachusetts native and a year-round resident of Martha's Vineyard. She and her husband of thirty-seven years are the parents of three adult children: Ryan, Tanya, and Rebecca. This is her first memoir.

ISLAND, A MEMOIR

"A masterful journey of transition honest, moving, and powerful a rich celebration of living on Martha's Vineyard in the middle years."

Nancy Aronie, Author, *Writing From the Heart*

"*Island* is the story of one woman's journey to find balance and peace. This book, with its clear and unpretentious style, is charming and delightful."

Carol L. Vega, Yoga Instructor

"Elaine has written a heartfelt love letter to the island of Martha's Vineyard. *Island* is both concise and lyrical—a testament to the charm of the Vineyard and to Elaine's appreciation of the island, of family, and of the up-and-down adventure of life itself."

John Hough, Jr., Author, *The Last Summer*

"Elaine takes midlife by the tail and introduces an act of chaos into her suburban existence...she reveals the joy, the mystery, and the struggle of starting anew—personally and professionally."

Debbie Phillips, Executive Coach, GroupMV

"Reading *Island* reconnected me with my own journey from a career-oriented life on the mainland to a life-oriented life on the Vineyard... *Island* brings the essence of Vineyard life into focus for the off-islander and reminds me of why I was drawn to make this amazing place my home."

Victoria Hanjian, Minister

ACKNOWLEDGEMENT

Special thanks to Ann Howes, a consummate artist, a member of the American Watercolor Society, and a long-time lover of the Vineyard, who provided the sketches to illustrate this memoir.

The vagrant wind

Slipped between my cracks

Swooped me up

And carried me to you

TABLE OF CONTENTS

PROLOGUE

"THEY ACCEPTED YOUR OFFER," the eager realtor's voice announces.

"They did? They didn't counteroffer?" I reply.

Six tumultuous months were ending with that call.

"A fast closing," the realtor adds. "They want to close quickly."

"Fine," I agree.

"Dan, Dan," I call to the driveway from the window of our New Jersey home, "they accepted the offer."

Then, the pall I had seen on his face so many times. Panic? Fear? Disappointment? What did that look mean this time? Had we not agreed that living near the ocean would be wonderful?

. . .

A year earlier I had quit my New Jersey job. It was time to change my life, I had decided. Then came the job offer from the Vineyard, the visits, the welcome, the idyllic setting. I accepted the job. But I had no idea what I was accepting.

I didn't know the difference then between a *Vineyarder*, an *off-islander*, and a *wash-ashore.* I had never experienced the fierce democracy that gives voice to every opinion, informed or not. Degrees, protocol, experience—all these were secondary to the Vineyard voices—the high-speed ferry voices, the wind farm voices, the golf course voices, the gas station voices, the voices entitled by land and heritage and kin to sing their spirited songs.

That voice on the telephone heralded the arrival of a cacophony of dissonant voices I might never have welcomed into my life had I known better. But at the time I didn't know better. I moved to the Vineyard, and there my story begins.

Chapter 1

ON THE ROAD

AUGUST. SIX CORMORANTS SIT ON LOGS in the harbor at the end of Walker Drive, Falmouth. One spreads its wings. Two eye the water, petulant, poised to fish. The other three are attentive but still. Across the water, seven miles away, is the island of Martha's Vineyard—my destination. Familiar territory? Not at all. I have spent the past twenty-five years in New Jersey.

The morning exodus from northern New Jersey on Route 287 and across the Tappan Zee Bridge is exhilarating at first. The four-lane Merritt Parkway, with its anachronistic tree-lined turns, provides familiar security. Not until I reach Route 95 in Stamford, Connecticut, do I hit the frenzy of neon and billboards and trucks with speeding tires spitting gravel.

Once I get past New Haven, I remind myself, much of the traffic will disperse. Past the exits to Madison and Clinton and Mystic Seaport and Niantic, I drive more serenely. Westerly and Stonington signal that I have reached Rhode Island. *Cape Cod*, directs the huge sign on the right in Providence. I navigate calmly for sixty more miles until the rotary leading onto the Bourne Bridge. *Stay in lane*, the bridge signs read. True, I think. Life is safer when we stay in our designated lanes.

Just do it, I tell myself. Still, I am reminded of the perils—a new life in a strange place, the loss of my professional networks and of old friends, departure from my lovely colonial home, newly renovated with the thought of avoiding extraordinary expenses in retirement only a few years away. I had raised three talented children in that New Jersey home. Dan, my husband, had been a good partner.

I've stopped analyzing what brought about this adventure.

Was it a failure of communication in my marriage—the small talk, the discord of different dreams?

Was it the human foibles I encountered daily in my professional life?

Was it the superficiality of friends or the recognition of how programmed all our lives had become?

Was it my yearning to live near the ocean?

Or was it something as simple as the realization that I had worked dutifully since I was fourteen years old and needed a change?

"I just don't get it," a friend said, exasperated. "Why would you do such a thing?"

"I'm not sure." I replied. "But I know that if I don't do it now, I never will."

Others were more direct. "Are you out of your mind? Some of those women look so weather-beaten. They don't even wear makeup."

Each member of my family reacted differently when I announced the move. "Go for it, Mom!" my son, the eldest, said. The older daughter, always cautious, feared the change. “You’re really going to do this, aren’t you, Mom?” the younger said. She was wise. For the past two years she had been sending her dad’s e-mails to him and mine separately to me. Her “Dear Mom” instead of “Dear Mom and Dad” had given me permission to forge my own identity after thirty-three years.

• • •

And here I am on the road, ready to become the principal of the West Tisbury School on Martha’s Vineyard.

Chapter 2

THE CELEBRATION

BEFORE I LEFT NEW JERSEY, I invited a group of women to celebrate my prospective adventure. Women from many parts of my life. Teachers. Former church friends. A dear neighbor, a fellow doctoral student. Reading club confidantes. Female administrators and a school board member. Mothers who, like me, possessed the self-knowledge we had reluctantly unearthed as we raised our children.

Each brought me a survival gift. These included books, wine, a scrapbook, wool socks, a first aid kit, a CD of sea sounds, and an English calligraphy blessing. The most unique gift was a set of postcards stamped and addressed to me. "Give these to your New Jersey friends, so you'll be sure to get lots of mail and you won't be lonely," my friend Jean told me.

Other gifts aimed to provide a spiritual boost or to direct me on my new path. Among them were a pocket book of Psalms and Proverbs and a logbook in which to record everything I ate or drank, and how much I exercised each day.

I opened most of these gifts after the guests had left. Each spoke vividly to me. They made me recall the days when I neglected to enjoy the beautiful sounds of nature, the days when I ate all the wrong things then punished myself by counting calories and fat grams, the days when my feet were cold because I didn't wear my wool socks, and the days when I forgot the prayers and blessings of friends.

• • •

Deep breath, I tell myself. Time to move on.

Chapter 3

ONWARD

ON THE MORNING OF AUGUST 1, my car and I pull into the fifth lane at the Woods Hole terminal. A lanky guitarist sits on the pavement, strumming, his backpack bulging with the provisions necessary for a Vineyard adventure. Energetic children peer from the open windows of their parents' SUVs, eating breakfast snacks and already asking, "How long 'til we're there?"

Some folks stand outside their cars, peering over the roofs and waiting for the waving arm of the Steamship Authority attendants who orchestrate the packing of fifty cars onto the *Islander*, the largest of the ferries.

Other folks look impatient. I imagine that they are tired from prevacation packing, from finishing that one last

The *Islander* Ferry

chore at work, from enduring heavy traffic at the approaches to the Bourne and the Sagamore Bridges. Others beam with anticipation. A Steamship Authority attendant and I chuckle at the family in the next car who refuses to drive the twenty-five yards from the parking lot into the boat until all four family members have buckled their seat belts. "Good luck on the Vineyard," the attendant offers.

"We're off," the ferry whistle bellows at exactly 8 a.m. The boat, packed with summer tourists, leaves the harbor at Woods Hole, passes the Elizabeth Islands, and ferries across Vineyard Sound and into the harbor at Tisbury. I am due at the office of the superintendent of schools at 9 a.m. My duties officially start today. I'm glad I'm on a tight schedule and have little time to ponder.

I remember how ambitious I was when, in New Jersey, I became a superintendent of schools myself. I have no regrets about the decision to leave that enervating position. The politics of warring local interest groups and the frustration of being managed by board members with no school experience had tired me. The longest of my superintendent days stretched continuously from 4 a.m. snow-closing calls to the adjournments of contentious board meetings when the gavel sounded at 3 a.m. At the end of such days, I had nothing better to write in my journal than "No time for teachers. No time for students. No time for learning today."

. . .

The superintendent of the Martha's Vineyard schools draws a profile of the challenges I will meet at the West Tisbury School, a place described by many as "very laid back." "The parents and kids love the place," he assures me. "So does the staff."

A school-choice policy allows nonresidents to attend the West Tisbury School from other towns on the island. Because the school is unique and popular, many do. Student achievement is good. I am expected to make it even better.

I walk energetically from the superintendent's office,

hopeful that, in this new place, I can focus on students and teachers and good programs rather than on politics and finances.

Chapter 4

THE TOPOGRAPHY

I NAVIGATE FARTHER UP ISLAND, leaving the more heavily settled Tisbury, founded in 1682, and drive past the Holmes Hole path, the site of the original mail route up the island. The Tashmoo Overlook on the right frames the harbor at which I arrived this morning.

Tashmoo Overlook, Vineyard Haven

Passing high-timbered oaks, beeches, and cedar, I see my surroundings change from the bustle of a commercial village to the rural tapestry of West Tisbury. Chicama Vineyards beckons with a wine tasting sign on the left; Nip and Tuck Farm offers flowers and vegetables and a prize-winning bull on the right. I haven't yet learned that the new Ag Hall was raised just a few years ago and is a symbol of pride to the local folk. I pass the old Ag Hall, the Grange, where farmers' and artists' markets are held weekly during the summer months.

South Road leads me past the Allen sheep farm, where I see the two styles of stone walls emblematic of Chilmark.

Stone Walls at Allen Sheep Farm in Chilmark

The words of Robert Frost, *something there is that doesn't love a wall,* take on a new meaning. These walls are works of art. Tightly meshed, some stand four feet tall and trace the perimeters of property on hillsides overlooking fields, ponds, and the Atlantic. Other stone walls are built with gaping holes. These were designed for the cattle and sheep to feed on the grasses on the other side. I think how helpful it would be if, as we built personal walls to protect ourselves, we left some holes for breathing and nourishment.

Beetlebung Corner is next. The beetlebung is the name of a local tree.

Nearby is the new Chilmark School, the subject of some consternation among the taxpayers of the up-island towns of West Tisbury, Chilmark, and Aquinnah. Built without state funds at the behest of the Chilmark locals, the costs of the school are supported by the taxpayers of the three up-island communities.

Over the next two years, the tiny Chilmark School will turn from a proud construction project to a source of endless challenges. Leaking roofs, rotting floorboards, a proliferation of mold and water problems will precipitate a vocal outcry from some West Tisbury folks. "Let them pay for their own problems. Why should we support a school with less than fifty students and all that trouble? Send them all to the West Tisbury School. Close that Chilmark School," some already chant.

Across the street from the Chilmark School, the vacant one-room Menemsha School reminds the locals of the way it used to be when the young children were educated there and the older children moved on to the down-island Tisbury School for their high school years. "I went to that school; many of us did," an islander later tells me proudly. "The classroom had four rows. One row for each grade. I remember the teacher. I learned fine. Look how I turned out. I did fine."

Continuing the drive on South Road takes me to the Gay Head Cliffs, the highest point on the island. Gay Head has been renamed Aquinnah to honor its Wampanoag heritage, but an errant sign here and there still reads with the old name. I stop in the driveway to the Chilmark School to meet those who arranged for my arrival.

Chapter 5

THE WELCOME

A VAN, A PICKUP TRUCK, AND FIVE PEOPLE greet me. Three mothers, a grandfather, and two students named Alex and Alex. "Follow me," one of the mothers says. "I'll lead you to Betsy's house." I drive farther along South Road and turn left onto Stonewall, a road marked by a bevy of mismatched mailboxes cocked at angles as though they are chatting with one another. Stonewall narrows to Moses West Trail then to Hill Land Lane.

Betsy is a stranger who knows little of me. One of the West Tisbury parents asked her to let me stay in her vacant cottage on Stonewall Pond until my year-round rental house becomes vacant. She agreed.

One room, the cottage is a gem. A bed, a small kitchen

corner, and a modest bath and laundry area punctuate the inside. Windows on one wall showcase Stonewall Pond. Windows on the second wall showcase the Chilmark section of the Atlantic, to be reached on foot by winding through conservation land pathways to the ocean. Windows on the third wall beckon me to a trail leading to kayaks to use on the pond.

"Just remember to use life jackets," Betsy says. She lives in a shingled home on the crest of the hill overlooking the ocean. I learn that the original owners of the home were lost in a hurricane. The house was saved.

Betsy's house is unlocked, as are most of the residences on the island. Its cozy rooms are framed by mahogany paneling and layered with shelves that hold black-and-white family photos and books. In front of a picture window overlooking the ocean is an antique writing desk. Betsy is an author. She lives in the unheated house until the first of November, then moves into the heated cottage, the place where I am to stay now, to spend the winter months.

"No problem, no problem," Betsy says as I thank her profusely for sharing her cottage with me. "No one is using it this month. It's yours." I like Betsy already.

"Oh, dear," worries Jane, one of the mothers, just before leaving me at Betsy's place. "I hope the ocean sounds don't keep you awake at night."

"That's an insomnia I'll welcome," I reply.

Last week, Jane e-mailed me in New Jersey and asked about my breakfast preferences so that she could stock the refrigerator. Very generous, I think to myself.

Susan, the second mother, photographs me in front of the cottage and then hurries down the road to her parents' family home to gather some dishes and a pot for cooking.

On a small collapsible shelf that serves as a table sit a vase of fresh gladioli, a box of Chilmark Chocolates, and a handwritten sign that says *Welcome, Elaine!* There is no phone, no TV, no cell phone reception. "This will be a retreat, a time to gather my thoughts," I muse. I vow to enjoy the rolling waves, the dune vistas, and the feel of the ocean winds on my skin in this idyllic setting.

Betsy invites me to stop in for coffee the next morning. "Any time after 5 a.m." she says. In the morning, as the sun rises across the dunes, we strangers talk for an hour. Betsy is a slim, energetic woman with a warm smile and wrinkles where the older smiles have been. I guess that she is near sixty. I learn that she is a hospice volunteer and works on the local first aid squad. She is about to depart with a group of friends to climb Mount Olympus. She is climbing to represent a friend who is ill and cannot make the climb herself.

Stonewall Beach

For the next fourteen nights, I navigate by moonlight to my solitary cottage.

Chapter 6

MISGIVINGS

ONE OF THE THINGS I realize about keeping a journal is that I don't write about the bad things. Particularly in such a pristine place as Martha's Vineyard, it feels wrong to paint the picture in less than its full glory. I'm learning that it's OK to admit my shortcomings and to acknowledge the foibles of the place.

I remember how I told my skeptical mother, "Mom, they don't have chain stores and malls on Martha's Vineyard!"

"Oh dear," she whispered, "I don't think I'd like that."

It took only a few days, however, for me to realize why the eighty-four-year-old had misgivings.

"Where's a dry cleaner?" I ask a neighbor.

"The dry cleaner is behind *The Black Dog* on State Road down island."

Down island during high tourist season means that a ten-minute drive can take a half hour on the island's meandering two-lane roads. "Forty-five miles per hour is the limit," one resident warns me, "and that's only on a few roads."

I travel down island to the dry cleaner and learn that my pantsuit will not return for a week. "A week!" I exclaim, remembering the "In by ten, out by five" service in New Jersey.

"Why, yes," the shopkeeper answers curtly. "We ship everything to Rhode Island. We don't have much industry here on the Vineyard. Don't like the chemicals."

I leave the pantsuit and drive back up island, amused at myself. Though I don't know it yet, it will be only a few months until I replace the spectator shoes and neatly pressed wool suits with boots and barn jackets and pants with billowy bottoms. One day, after six months on the job, three fifth grade students eye me curiously and announce, "You look like a regular person today!"

Chapter 7

WHAT PRICE BEAUTY?

END OF PUBLIC BEACH. NO TRESPASSING, warns the sign in Lambert's Cove. I later find a similar sign at Great Rock Bight. Many others dot the island. I'm not sure how I feel about this.

The placid beauty and the drama of the island are directly related to its limited access. Ongoing battles rage between the Steamship Authority and those who want high-speed ferries to promote easier access to the Vineyard. "We certainly don't want to be like Nantucket," some Vineyarders assert. "Too commercial!"

"Tell New Bedford to send their fast ferry somewhere else," others protest.

Months after my arrival, an application for a new golf

course is perceived as a threat to the environment in the Southern Woodlands section of Oak Bluffs and is vetoed by the Martha's Vineyard Commission. The owner of the land, the person who proposed the golf course, retaliates by cutting down fields of trees in the treasured setting. The bird lovers and the naturalists and the environmentalists and the locals are enraged. The feud continues.

Water-view parcels of land, selling at bargain prices of more than a million dollars, remind me that only an incredible act of generosity on Betsy's part gives me the opportunity to swim in the Atlantic at the private Stonewall Beach. Betsy's unheated home and her winter one-room cottage are not ostentatious at all. They are humble, weather-shingled tributes to the vistas all around.

Vineyarders must constantly address the problem of making the beauty accessible without destroying the landscape. Critical questions are posed. Do we plan for affordable housing so that people of modest means can continue to enrich the population of Martha's Vineyard? Or do we control the zoning so strictly that only the wealthiest can afford to live on the island?

I re-read what I have just written. I realize that I have used the subject "we." Am I starting to feel the passion of this place?

Many volunteers promote conservation efforts. Island leader Kate Warner spearheads efforts to educate Vineyard residents so that they understand that their natural resources are finite. She brings speakers from Denver, Denmark, and Seattle to help the natives understand how other island folk cope with similar challenges. Solar power, wind turbines, recycling of resources. I realize that I'm recycling a life too.

A local Land Bank assesses a fee of two percent on the purchase price of all real estate transactions, and that money (seventy million dollars so far) has been used to protect more than three thousand acres unto perpetuity. Those three thousand acres trail across the island and defend the gnarled oaks, the ancient trails, the tranquil grasslands, the sanctuaries and wildlife refuges, and the coastal pond ecosystems.

I remember the New Jersey beaches, jukeboxes and plastic picnics and trashcans and teeming life. I decide that limited access and protection of natural resources has its benefits.

Chapter 8

STARTING TO EXPLORE

AT THE BUNCH OF GRAPES BOOKSTORE, I buy a book called *Hiking Trails of Martha's Vineyard.* Today I am hiking the Great Rock Bight trail past Marl Pond and through an ancient field to a Vineyard Sound beach, where I will sit to write.

Great Rock Bight, West Tisbury

En route, I pass a small stone memorial for Rebecca, wife of a man named Abel of the Wampanoag Tribe. "She came to Chilmark from Africa as a slave," the memorial says. "She died free in 1801." She, a former slave, found a home, a spouse, a family, and ultimately her freedom on Martha's Vineyard. What will I find?

Most dramatic is what I do not find. No more breakneck commutes on Interstate 80. No more traffic jams. No junk mail for weeks. No cell phone service. Nightly returns to my whimsical cottage at the end of a mile of dirt roads take some courage at first, especially with no neighbors. But as the rabbits scatter near the front door of the cottage and the waves pound a welcome, I adjust.

I hear that many come to the Vineyard to escape from various kinds of slavery. "On this island," one person tells me, "you'll find roofers and electricians and fishermen who hold PhDs. It's a quality of life thing."

For years I felt a nagging ache, a vague longing, a hint that life might be better. But with three children to raise, a husband to befriend, a doctorate to earn, and several jobs to master, I neglected to search until now.

Chapter 9

POSSIBLE DREAMS

FOUR HUNDRED THOUSAND DOLLARS. Imagine it.

Not even ten days into my time on the Vineyard, I attend the annual celebrity auction called *Possible Dreams.* "You won't believe it," a friend says. "You go to the courtyard of the Harborside Inn in Edgartown. You sit right next to celebrities who are giving away good deeds, not things. You don't buy an antique plate; you buy a sail with Walter Cronkite. Or you buy a chance to record with Carly Simon. Or you buy a Bill Smith clambake on the beach."

It sounds like a good opportunity to get an inside view of a Vineyard tradition. I go.

Driving into Edgartown during the summertime is a challenge. I park outside of town and walk in. Edgartown's streets of white clapboard homes with trim black shutters are testament to the town's proud historic character. The Old Whaling Church sits next door to the Preservation Society, which meticulously preserves the antique décor and furnishings popular two hundred years earlier. A few blocks farther, outside the historical museum, stands a lighthouse that retains its crystal lamp. Some of the homes have a widow's walk, a place from which the wives of sea captains and fishermen would scan the seas for the return of their loved ones from ill-fated sea journeys.

I reach North Water Street, the site of the Harborside Inn. Not until I find the hotel courtyard packed with folks squeezing in wherever they can find space do I understand why everyone has told me to bring a chair. Fishermen, school secretaries, nurses, real estate agents, locals and tourists, unfold portable chairs, socialize, or just watch and wait. Beauty and fame punctuate the place.

Close enough to shake my hand are Walter Cronkite, Carly Simon, Art Buchwald, Mike Wallace, David McCullough. The same Walter Cronkite I remember broadcasting the death of President Kennedy. The same Carly Simon I remember playing and singing to my first two children more than twenty years ago. I can hear her voice: "*Winken, Blinken, and Nod one night sailed off in a wooden shoe.*" Months later, when I tell her how I loved that album, she says it was her first. "I recorded it with my sister Lucy," she tells me.

Most moving, though, is Art Buchwald, the master of ceremonies at the *Possible Dreams* auction. This auction marks his return after a debilitating stroke. Words slurred but spirit strong, Buchwald delights the audience with quips, one liners, and the same humor that had me laughing out loud reading his syndicated columns twenty years ago.

But the best is Carly Simon. She is auction item number 34. Wearing a striped top and sunglasses, she stands at the front of the courtyard. Shouts come from every corner.

"Five grand."

"Twelve grand."

"Seventeen grand."

Then twenty, twenty-two, and thirty grand. At that, Carly belts out *You're So Vain*. The audience bursts into applause.

"Forty thousand."

"Forty-two."

Nobody Does It Better, Carly offers next.

"Sing *Jesse*," someone shouts from the middle of the courtyard.

Jesse it was.

The bidding reaches $55,000.

Let the River Run.

When Carly sings about the new Jerusalem, I for a moment imagine that I have found mine.

Some tell me that this is the real spirit of the Vineyard. Not the rich and famous to be admired from outside their mansion security gates by those in a tour bus. Here the rich and famous gather in the courtyard and give their talent and fortune back to the beautiful island. This year's auction deposits $403,600 into the community service coffers.

Chapter 10

OLD HABITS

DURING MY FIRST DAYS IN THE COTTAGE, I conscientiously draw the blinds as I undress. Later I laugh at myself. Is there really someone in this remote place who would lust in the dark after a fifty-something body? I stop drawing the blinds.

Another habit I must unlearn is locking my car. New friends Sarah and John invite me for dinner. I arrive at half-past five after winding down unmarked dirt roads in Chilmark. John and Rufus, the dog, meet me in the driveway. "I'll be right in," John says, as I join Sarah to chat while she prepares the meal. Midway through dinner, John tactfully offers, "Elaine, you don't need to lock your car doors here." I realize the folly of locking the doors in the middle of these woods. I give myself permission to leave my car unlocked when I park it.

Work is a habit too. Neither Dan nor I come from families where college educations and jobs have anything to do with personal fulfillment. Work is the only goal. Fulfillment is a matter of pure luck. Our mandates were always clear. For the men, the purpose of work was to support a family. For women, work outside the home ended when children arrived, and resumed only when they no longer needed their mother's doting and care. That was the way of the pre-baby boomers.

. . .

So what's left after the children are raised, the college educations paid, and the professional achievements mastered? This is not the story of a romantic interlude or of a dropout from marriage or even of retirement. This is the story of someone who realized that old habits can be undone just as the running shoe that pounds the pavements can be unlaced and put away.

Chapter 11

MOVING ON

UNTIL I DECIDED TO MOVE TO THE VINEYARD, I had never thought of undoing habits, of changing the patterns in my life, of moving on. Certainly moving on had not occurred to me on a scale of going out of state. It had not occurred to me that I could leave one geographic region and move to another at this stage in my life. It certainly had not occurred to me that I would do this alone.

Moving itself wasn't new to me. I had often relocated through my jobs, maintaining the demeanor of the happy mom and the faithful wife in a sleepy New Jersey suburb. I realize now the indoctrination in the words of old songs I heard as a child. *Pretend you're happy when you're blue. Smile though your heart is aching. Whistle a happy tune and no one will suspect you're afraid.*

No one suspected I wasn't happy. Plumbing new job opportunities, I moved on every three to five years to a new spot, to a better opportunity, to a higher income, whistling and smiling all the while. I worked hard to nurture my family, my colleagues, my employees. I knew well how to nurture others. I had no idea how to nurture myself.

• • •

I think of the title of a popular book: *Wherever You Go, There You Are*. This time, I will leave some things behind. I can't care for myself with so much baggage to carry. The simplicity and unpretentiousness of the Vineyard will help.

I think of the empty boxes left at the local dump off the Edgartown-West Tisbury road. The boxes once were meticulously packed and padded to preserve old treasures. Boxes labeled *fragile*. Boxes marked with arrows so that they would remain upright. Wardrobe boxes that held tuxes and chiffon evening wear. Underbed boxes used to hide away what didn't fit in the drawers. All those boxes, flattened and ready for recycling.

What do I really need, I ask myself, as I move on?

Chapter 12

QUESTIONS

IN OUR MARRIAGE I WAS ALWAYS THE DREAMER. The familial script "When will you be satisfied?" was echoed by my mother, then by my husband. "Why move?" he would ask. "This New Jersey house is solidly built and everything works fine. Besides, we put a lot of money into remodeling."

When parents plant the *do your best and strive to get A's* philosophy, they rarely project into the distant future. Once the years of honor rolls and deans lists are over, children don't easily shake off the *be the best* mentality. We don't question the stakes of getting A's as life goes on. We blame foreigners for the tragedy of 9/11, but do we examine ourselves when the excesses of Enron become public, when the Martha Stewarts meet their demise? What options do we choose when we get a choice? What is the price of those A's?

I hear an amusing story about the time when the town of Tisbury was planning to renovate its library. I'm told that for months hearings were held so that citizens could give input, review architectural designs, and be sure that the projected library would meet the needs of the community. At the end of the examination of all the options, the new library was built. A huge protest ensued. Members of the community found the large columns at the entrance distasteful—the same columns that had been on the architectural designs since the original drawings. The columns had to be dismantled and the newly built façade redesigned.

It's important to ask the right questions.

I am grateful to Dan that he did not treat my questions and my conclusions as a threat to him or to our marriage, although they might have been.

I remember the dismal words of friends who were already anticipating the ending of the story. "Sad, this is so sad," a few said. "After thirty-three years of marriage! Sad."

I sit writing this on a September Sunday, with the ocean

breaking less than twenty feet away, but with my husband twenty-times-twenty miles away.

Chapter 13

LIBERATION

THE WOMAN PASSING ME AT THE POST OFFICE is lanky and muscular. Her long, mouse-brown hair is dappled with grey and resembles the tail of a workhorse. At the counter are three other women. Two also have long hair—one a ponytail, the other a French braid. The third wears a fresh boy cut. A blond woman enters, clearly a tourist. You can tell by the highlights, the two-process dye job, the French manicure, and the red-nailed pedicure poking from the stylish sandals. Here on the Vineyard I've let my hair go curly, no longer blowing and brushing and masking its nature.

I'm told that women here are strong. I meet one who runs a bed and breakfast all by herself. I mean really all by herself—no cleaning person, no handyman, no cook. She bakes bread every day. She invites me for tea. Cinnamon raisin toast, cheeses, cucumber sandwiches, miniature orange and poppy seed loaves. This woman is delightful.

• • •

My generation was lured by a repertoire of half-truths about women.

Women can do anything men can.
Household jobs should be equitably shared.
Roles can easily be reversed, partnerships adjusted.
Women should work outside the home.
Sons should do dishes as well as daughters.
Glass ceilings can be broken.

None of these statements is false. None, though, is entirely true.

And all come with consequences. If I were to assemble truths to communicate to my grandchildren, I would tell them that the 1960s, consciousness-raising and revolutionary as they were, did not effectively redefine women's roles. Outspoken demonstrations, sexual promiscuity, experimenting with drugs, burning of bras—few of these social outcries changed women's lives in any significant way. More than forty years later, women still struggle to balance the yin and yang in their lives. *Title IX* gave federal clout to the entitlements of women, but equal opportunity acts are still not law in many states.

• • •

I leave the post office after mailing a letter to a city friend.

"You should come," I invite her. "You'll like it here."

Chapter 14

REWARDS

I AM SURPRISED WHEN SOME PEOPLE DESCRIBE ME as bright. I don't think of myself that way. Skilled? Maybe. Experienced? Yes. Hardworking, definitely. Bright? Not so sure.

But when I was younger, I valued being smart. Progress was linear. My mantras were achievement, clear goals, hard work. Once you accomplish goal A, you go on to goal B. Dedication to hard work gives you the license to tackle even harder work. Certificates, plaques, and ceremonies pay tribute to those who chant these mantras.

Imagine my surprise when I arrived at the West Tisbury School and learned that there are no grades, no distinctions, few competitions between students. The West

Tisbury School is the only school on the island without an honor roll. I enjoy standing outside the school in the mornings and watching the children emerge from their buses. I notice, when my first year at the West Tisbury School is over, that the students arrive and depart just as happily in June as they did in September. And many of the school's former graduates number in the top twenty to graduate from the high school each year. Does the absence of rankings and rewards in the early years contribute to student confidence and healthy development in the long run? Many think so.

Periodically I deal with the chagrin of a few off-island parents who insist that our standards are too low. "Can't you make them give more homework?" they ask.

Occasionally parents criticize the teachers themselves. "She teaches absolutely no science," one complains. "My son likes science. We bought him a science kit for Christmas. He's learning nothing in her class."

"You're not doing your job," another parent attacks. "You're the principal. Do your job. I want to see bumper stickers that say, *My child is an honor student at the West Tisbury School.*"

I try to explain the difference between intrinsic and extrinsic rewards. The parent isn't listening. She departs in a huff with the words, "Private school is the only answer. I'm disappointed, Dr. Pace, I'm really disappointed."

I think of the many years I was driven by rewards, by the external expectations of others. I believe that my new path is healthy and life affirming. Still, some days are more rewarding than others.

Chapter 15

METROPOLIS

WEST TISBURY HAS ELEVEN MILES OF PAVED public roads and many miles of dirt roads with more ruts and potholes than an ordinary life. Today I rumble down Old Courthouse Road past the old fire station. If I turn left, I come to Humphreys. Old Bart Humphrey (who has now passed away) would often sit at one of the three tables in the bakery and hold court with the seasoned citizens. Mike and Donna Diaz run Humphreys, home of the best tomato-mozzarella sandwich I've had anywhere.

At the end of Old Courthouse Road, I turn right and head toward Cronig's Up Island Market. I pass the road to Christiantown, an early island settlement that borders some of the most stunning north shore trails on the island. West Tisbury, the largest town, is held in place on the north shore by Vineyard Sound and on the south shore by the Atlantic Ocean.

Mrs. Blake's Pies, Cobalt Gallery, the Martha's Vineyard Cooperative Bank, Vineyard Gardens, and The Martha's Vineyard Wellness Center mark the mile between Old Courthouse Road and Cronig's Market. Wayne Blake of Mrs. Blake's Pies sits, every day of the summer and many days of the off-season, in his homemade wooden booth in front of his modest ranch home, and greets those who yearn for the peach-blueberry, cranberry, and chocolate-chip pies baked by his wife and daughter. Two or three times daily, one of the women emerges from the house and trucks thirty or forty steaming new pies to the booth. Peach-blueberry is my favorite. I hand Mr. Blake eleven dollars, the advertised price of the pie. He returns one of the bills. I look quizzically. "You're an islander," he replies. "Eleven dollars is for the tourists."

Funny how simply things are named here. Here is Cronig's Up Island Market. Its counterpart is Cronig's Down Island Market. The parallel roads between here and Aquinnah, the highest elevation on the island, are called North, Middle, and South. The connecting roads between Edgartown and Vineyard Haven and Edgartown and West Tisbury are Edgartown-Vineyard Haven Road and Edgartown-West Tisbury Road.

The West Tisbury Postoffice

I don't drive to Cronig's Up Island Market for groceries on this day, though. I have come for my mail. I am proud to have gone through a first rite of passage. I am no longer *Pace, General Delivery*. I am now *Pace, P.O. Box 1346*. I no longer ask for my mail at the counter. I have a key of my own. The post office box and key, however, don't guarantee any confidentiality.

"Hey, Elaine, where've you been?" asks Little Dave when I neglect to pick up my mail for a few days. Little Dave is six feet tall. His work partner, Big Dave, is the same height. Tony helps me today. Tony also owns a popular Vineyard restaurant in Edgartown, The Square Rigger.

During my first year on the Vineyard, Big Dave, Little

Dave, and Tony shepherd my mail and packages. "Looks like you got some coffee again," announces Little Dave as my Starbucks shipment arrives. And, on another day, "Order some CDs?"

"What'd you get?" inquires a friendly stranger behind me in line.

"*Songbird*, by Eva Cassidy," I reply. "I heard a song featured on WMVY. Loved it." Meanwhile James Taylor music plays in the background at the post office. His mother and other relatives still live on the island. James Taylor is a native son.

The West Tisbury post office is a microcosm of the island. Many women are sun-crossed, with leathery faces. They wear hiking boots with heavy socks. On this island, nylon stockings and heavy eye shadow are as scorned as those who haven't taken up composting and recycling. Good thing I don't wear much makeup, I think to myself. One of the Vineyard women I see today, a tall, attractive blonde, drives a heavy front loader at the local recycling center.

The ponytails and long hair aren't relegated to the women in this metropolis. Many men wear the same style. After a few months, I become used to meeting poets and writers who do construction work for their day jobs and who gather daily at the heavy wooden picnic tables next door to the post office and eat egg sandwiches, calzones, and pizza slices from Biga Bakery. Doug and Beth own Biga. I meet Beth in my yoga class. She bakes through the night and celebrates when Biga closes during January and February. Once in a while, Beth brings a plate of fresh cookies or peanut-butter brownies for us to sample after yoga class.

One day I go to Biga during a crowded lunch hour. I order calzone with sausage. "Your yoga teacher wouldn't be happy to see you eating that," Doug, the owner, chastises me from the grill at the back of the store.

"Oh, my," I sigh that day as I slink out the side door quickly before everyone turns to see who the non-vegetarian is.

Courage and independence mark many Vineyard women. At a rehearsal of the All-Island Chorus, I meet Claudia, just back from a solitary adventure on the back roads of Maine. Betsy recently returned from her hike to the top of Mount Olympus and is en route to explore Taos, New Mexico. A cohort of sixty-something women swim in Lambert's Cove daily at dawn all summer. The West Tisbury police chief is a woman. She replaced an icon, longtime chief George Manter, and that was no easy task. I replaced another icon, Bob Tankard, a former coach and a much-beloved principal. That was no easy task either.

Many women are successful living life solo and working in this metropolis.

Chapter 16

HOMELESS

AFTER MY FIRST TWO WEEKS ON STONEWALL POND, I move to the West Tisbury house that I will rent for the next ten months. A new structure, it is light, cheery, and welcoming. Living in the one-room cottage prepares me for this eight-hundred-square-foot house of two tiny bedrooms and a bright family/kitchen area. I am content.

I am content, that is, until the reality of finding a permanent home on the Vineyard begins to sink in. For four months, I plumb real estate opportunities and wait for housing prices to drop, as they seem to be doing everywhere else. But each time I find a place with promise, it sells at, or near, asking price. The price of a place half the size of our New Jersey home is double in cost here.

I think of my New Jersey home. "An acre of privacy on a beautifully wooded lot. Four bedrooms, master bath with Jacuzzi, comfortable family room, formal dining room, living room with fireplace, airy porch," the real estate sales brochure read.

Dan visits and continues the house search with me on weekends. Our frustrations over the real estate complications translate into frustrations with each other. Pragmatic, Dan secretly hopes I will come to my senses and return to New Jersey. In response, I become even more determined to make this new life work.

We abandon house hunting and try land hunting. We find a beautiful lot on a county road near the West Tisbury School and, for several weeks, negotiate to buy it. A visit to a local architect, however, convinces me that, by the end of the building project, we will spend more money than if we buy a completed home. Building a house on the Vineyard, the architect explains, takes one to two years. And that will happen only if local workmen are available. That's a rarity, she tells me.

Soon I learn that there will be no turning back. Dan, who has worked in the same company for the past twenty-three years and has made no attempt to change jobs, suddenly procures two job offers, one in the Providence area and one in Boston. I find myself leaving the Vineyard regularly to help him to find a new place to live near whichever job he decides to accept. Our energies are diverted to analyzing the benefits of each of his opportunities. The Martha's Vineyard home search takes a distant fourth place to these other decisions.

I fight the tendency to feel sorry for myself. I can't dismiss the fact that once again the husband's welfare dominates the direction of a marriage. Had I had a crystal ball, I would have realized that the job change for Dan would make it possible for us both to have a home on the Vineyard.

The hues of our lives begin to brighten. Dan starts work in Boston in January of 2002, five months after I move to the Vineyard. He finds a studio apartment to rent in Cambridge, then commutes to the Vineyard on weekends as do many other Vineyard folk. One week after Dan begins work in Cambridge, we finalize the purchase of our new Martha's Vineyard home. We hope the New Jersey home will sell.

The new Vineyard home is in a community we had rejected at first sight. Forty homes later, however, we realize that Deep Bottom Pond will provide us with light, solace, and a nesting place for the New Jersey possessions worthy of the move.

Chapter 17

LOCAL PRIDE

"WHAT TOWN DID YOU CHOOSE?" some ask, when they know we have bought a house. At first I only knew the geography, but now I am beginning to know the personalities of the towns.

Martha's Vineyard is an island much larger than most people suspect. It is comprised of six unique towns. Vineyard Haven (also called Tisbury), Oak Bluffs, and Edgartown are called the down-island towns. West Tisbury, Chilmark, and Aquinnah are the up-island towns. Menemsha, the picturesque fishing village, is a part of Chilmark, although their cultures are as different from each other as are the cultures of the other up- and down-island towns.

Aquinnah, marked by its majestic cliffs, has a proud tradition as the home of the Wampanoag tribe of Native

Americans. Rich in culture, the Wampanoags revel in their folk stories, their dance, their rituals, and their community. Occasional zoning disputes mar the relationship between the Wampanoags and other Aquinnah residents, but what's an island without some drama?

Gay Head Cliffs, Aquinnah

Chilmark holds the paradoxical distinction of having one of the highest per-capita incomes in the commonwealth of Massachusetts and one of the lowest tax rates. The Chilmark vistas of rolling farmland, grazing sheep, and ocean backdrops remind me of Scotland. Some roads have droll names like Half-Inch Lane. Sounds like a road where the Lilliputians might have lived. The names of other byways—Osprey Lane and Cygnet Way and Blue Heron Lane—tell of the wildlife someone once saw there. Still other names hint at who lived or walked the roads—

Doctor's Cove, Shepherd's Path. I pass Tea Lane. Tea Lane is marked as the site of pre-Revolutionary consumption of contraband tea.

The *up* and the *down* that distinguish the up- and down-island towns are directly related to topology and altitude, although some may think otherwise. The island has six town governments with six sets of selectmen, six local school boards, six zip codes, and six gas stations. I get to know the towns not through maps and guides but through conversations and interactions.

The huge white oil drums that greet the ferries traveling into Vineyard Haven supply the gas stations across the island. Gas stations are the hot topic of local news for months as a group of entrepreneurs applies to open a new one. The permits are completed, the feasibility studies done, the reports delivered, the economies iterated, and the vote taken by the Martha's Vineyard commissioners, the group that attempts to regulate the six diverse island towns.

No new gas station, they vote.

"But why?" many ask. "We need another gas station, and besides, the new place will offer gas at lower prices."

"We have environmental concerns. Besides, those island

folks have been around a long time," is the answer. "We don't want to hurt their business."

The feud continues.

. . .

"You look like you work in Edgartown," Sue, the office secretary, says to me one day in a cryptic voice that catches my attention.

"Why?" Sue has lots of EQ, emotional intelligence. I have learned to pay close attention to her.

"Those are Edgartown colors," she replies curtly.

I look down at my outfit. Navy slacks and vest, green turtleneck. "Edgartown colors?"

"Yeah, they wear those colors at the yacht club. Don't wear those colors," says Sue, who comes to work barefoot.

. . .

Proprietary feelings permeate every inch of the island. "Can you imagine repaving the sidewalks of Vineyard Haven and not using bricks?"

"But we don't want to look like Edgartown."

"Why not? Edgartown looks great."

"We're Vineyard Haven. We don't need to waste money on cosmetics. Cement sidewalks will be fine."

It doesn't take me long to learn that coming to consensus is a rarity on the Vineyard. The Vineyard isn't a place for those who dislike conflict.

Vineyard Haven and the up-island towns are dry.

"Go to dinner there and you bring your own wine. Saves money," some say. "And keeps the riff-raff away."

"Can you imagine not even being able to buy a drink?" others deride. "Those towns are no fun at all!" How Oak Bluffs, with its wonderful Methodist campground of a century ago, welcomed alcohol would be interesting to learn. I learn later that alcoholism is the most serious health problem in all the island towns, dry or not.

In Oak Bluffs, gingerbread cottages surround the outdoor tabernacle still used for patriotic Fourth of July concerts and other events. White latticework edges the roofs of the cottages, which are painted in ice-cream hues of pink and lavender and yellow-green. On *Illumination Night* in August, the latticed roofs are laced with tiny white lights that transfigure the Oak Bluffs campground into an enchanted place equal to any that Disney might create. I recall how Illumination Night fueled my romantic hopes of this island during my first summer on the island.

Over time, my romanticism tempers considerably.

"Will you stay?" some ask. "Many people stay one, two, three years and that's it. Just can't take the island ways."

"Yes, I'm staying," I reply, but not always convincingly.

Chapter 18

DOORS AND WINDOWS

THE VINEYARD EXPERIENCE IS A FORAY into the meaning of doors and windows.

DOORS. The longer I live here, the more secure I feel with less security. Where else in the world does the grocery delivery man walk right into the house and put the groceries away in the refrigerator, whether we are home or not? Where else in the world does the UPS man open the front door and tuck the package into the hallway? How about the neighbor who enters through the side door and the basement and up the stairs to the kitchen? "What are those footsteps?" we wonder, until we identify the "intruder."

I recall when a teacher at my school was hit in her car by a pickup truck whose driver sped away. After a quick scan of the island, the police alerted the Steamship Authority and the culprit was handily captured as he attempted to exit the ferry in Woods Hole. Doors wide open, coming and going.

WINDOWS. One of the things I like best about our new house is its airiness, its floor-to-ceiling windows, its embracing of the outside from within. I recall the month of recuperation from foot surgery in February of 2004. I lounged on the sofa, warmed by an enthusiastic fire and calmed by the sylvan setting outside.

Our former New Jersey home was lovely, but it was dark and secretive. This house is open to the world, for better or for worse.

Chapter 19

ROUTINES

MY HUSBAND DAN IS A MAN OF ROUTINE. He is a morning person. He represents thirty-three years of coffee on, dog out, shave, scrub, floss, off to work, home from work, eat with kids, coach or volunteer, read a bedtime story to the youngest, set out morning clothes, go to bed. This man of routine has altered his routine seamlessly.

Dan's hour-long New Jersey auto commute has been transposed to a five-minute ride to work in Cambridge on the T, Boston's underground transit system. The new routine includes a weekly flight to and from Martha's Vineyard to be with me on weekends.

Dan leaves Boston's Logan Airport at 6 p.m. every Friday, occupies one of nine seats on a Cape Air puddle jumper, and arrives on the Vineyard around 6:28, depending upon how long the miniature plane sits at Logan. The Cape Air plane looks like a toy, dwarfed between the jumbo jets on the runway.

. . .

I once made the mistake of taking a Cape Air flight from the Vineyard to Boston when the wind was forty miles per hour. "OK, folks," the pilot announced. "We have a little wind today, so hold on." Eyes shut, I practiced my Lamaze breathing techniques more passionately than I ever did during the births of my three babies.

. . .

I pick Dan up at the Martha's Vineyard Airport a mile from our house and return him on Monday morning at 6 a.m. It doesn't take me long to realize that I can make the trip directly out of bed and wearing pajamas and slippers with a coat when I need it. I feel empowered with this freedom. I remember how, in New Jersey, I habitually checked my hair and lipstick and outfit before going to the corner store.

On Friday nights when Dan arrives we share some favorite routines. Sometimes we come home to a candlelight dinner of freshly caught fish and a salad. Sometimes we go to

Lattanzi's for a pizza. Sometimes we pick up a deep dish pizza at Louis's and eat it by the fire with a glass of zinfandel. Sometimes I drive to Grace Church in Vineyard Haven and buy lobster rolls and slices of pie baked by the church women. Often, my friend Casey spots me and stuffs our rolls extra full. Then I head to the airport, pick up Dan, and we drive to the public beach at Menemsha for a sunset picnic. It's hard to find a parking space, but the effort is worth it. Some say that the sunset at Menemsha is the most beautiful on the East Coast. We love the cheer of the sunset seekers each time the fiery ball finally collapses beneath the horizon and the remaining embers tint the sky until dark comes.

Chapter 20

OLD FRIEND

JOY AND I have been friends since our daughters, now each thirty-one, were Brownie Scouts together. She forged new directions herself when she and her husband decided to leave Kinnelon, our New Jersey town, to move to a new home closer to his Trenton work place. The tradeoff for Joy was that she would be able to fulfill a lifelong dream: studying at Princeton Theological Seminary to become a minister.

Joy and I communicate only a few times each year, but we remain close. When Joy's mother dies, she asks if she can visit me on the Vineyard. "I need a retreat," she says, "a quiet place to pray and reflect while you are at work. I'll do dinners and we can spend the evenings together."

Joy's visit bridges the chasm between New Jersey and Massachusetts. She brings books, opera music, good recipes, and the solace of a nonjudgmental friend. Each day when I come home from work, *La Traviata* serves as the backdrop to our dinners and conversations, which run late into the night. I wonder if, in time, I will develop such friendships here on this island.

Chapter 21

SCHOOL

THE FIRST YEAR of my work at the West Tisbury School ends. As I think back on this first year, I realize that this principalship has involved many unexpected challenges that started with the events of September 11, 2001. Many years of handling school crises, from deaths to fires and financial demise, gave me the internal menu to deal with 9/11. Turn off the TVs, stay in close touch with the teachers, calm the parents, work with the crisis response personnel, talk to the students, communicate empathetically but clearly. As the day ended, I realized that in the years ahead people will ask, "Where were you when the towers collapsed?" just as they asked "Where were you when Kennedy died?" It is sad to be a part of this history.

. . .

The school I inherited is curiously linked to the 1960s in its iconoclasm and its promise of hope for the future.

"How do you like the nuts and granola school?" one retired teacher from another town asks sardonically at a Vineyard barbecue. "In the seventies, they took down all the walls. They go barefoot there."

"Imagine," several off-islanders and a few newly registered parents exclaim, "they call teachers by their first names! I hope you'll be changing that."

I smile, knowing that the locals will call this parent a *wash-ashore*, never a *Vineyarder*, not even an *off-islander*. That is the gradation of acceptance. Being a *Vineyarder* is best. But if you arrive from elsewhere, even if that arrival happened a half-century ago, you are an *off-islander*. If, however, you disparage the culture of the place, you'll forever be a *wash-ashore*. I pray that I can remain at least an *off-islander*, but I fear that I have approached *wash-ashore* status more than a few times during this first school year.

Probably the closest I have come to being pegged a *wash-ashore* was when I begin a campaign to improve punctuality at the school. Little did I know that my winsome war on tardiness would unleash such venom. "That's what I love about the West Tisbury School," one parent complained vociferously. "It doesn't matter what time you get your kids there, as long as they come. You're going to ruin the culture of the place!" She stormed out with her touch-tone finger ready to punch out several complaining calls to her friends and neighbors.

Others were more subtle. One sweet sixth grader approached me as I stood outside at dismissal time. "Why do you want us to come on time?" he queried innocently. "Our teacher tells us you want us to come on time." "Ah," I thought, "there's sabotage afoot."

In New Jersey, nothing for an administrator would be more fundamental than urging the students and parents to arrive at school on time. I realize that twenty-five years of experience in education still hasn't prepared me for this place.

By December of that first year, I knew that I had to bridge the gap between my concept of school culture and that of the West Tisbury School. I issued an open invitation to members of the faculty to join me on a school leadership team. Seven outstanding professionals responded. I accepted them all. Warm, bright, and nonpolitical, these professionals cared about the welfare of the school, of the children, and of education. Weekly from January to June, we had breakfast meetings. The team generated good ideas, introduced professional literature, and was open to discussing research and the structure of other kinds of schools. Most important, they provided the direct and unambiguous feedback I desperately needed. "Go for it," they sometimes said. "Cool it," sometimes. And sometimes, "It really doesn't matter." I am grateful for these unadulterated professionals who are confident enough to face the chagrin of some of their colleagues as they team with the new principal. During my three years at the school, twelve different professionals work with me on the school leadership team.

Most staff members are warm and welcoming. But I am unaccustomed to the scrutiny, the lack of trust, and the immediacy of some to jump to negative conclusions about my leadership. In retrospect, I realize that the adjustment may not have as much to do with me as with the slow change in the culture of the school itself. The noncompetitive mantra of the school clashes with the driven goals of families from high-powered school districts across the nation. An ageing local taxpayer population questions the return on the dollars required to support education in West Tisbury and in the Up-Island Regional School District to which the West Tisbury School belongs. My arrival coincides with many of these conflicts.

I didn't do my research on the place. Lured by the romanticism of twenty years of national seashore vacations on Cape Cod, I assumed that Martha's Vineyard would be as idyllic as our summer family vacations had been. My last principalship had been productive and gratifying. Why would this one be any different?

Gnarled Oak

Chapter 22

REAL PEOPLE

MEDIA MADNESS CONVINCES US that famous folk are different from the rest of us. I learn otherwise the longer I live here on the Vineyard.

When a friend comes to visit, I take her to The Galley, a local eatery in the village of Menemsha. "It's Michael J. Fox!" she notices. He is reading a newspaper and waiting for his food in the outdoor picnic area behind The Galley. His wife and children are with him. "Can I ask for his autograph?" she asks.

"I wouldn't," I reply.

We drive from Menemsha, past Alley's General Store, with its message board advertising *fly swatters*, to The Granary Gallery in West Tisbury. Two people chat in front of an oil painting of a rustic knotty pine bedroom with mosquito netting tied above the two twin beds. "That's where the Clintons sleep when they're here," one says to the other.

"Oh, really. Interesting," I overhear.

Alley's General Store, West Tisbury

We drive down island to meet a fisherman who takes us out in his boat along the shoreline from Tashmoo to Edgartown.

"That's Diane Sawyer's house," he notes. "I did some work there once. It's a comfortable, unassuming place."

My friend is wide-eyed.

We ride past the drawbridge in Tisbury, along the harbor in Oak Bluffs, and on to Herring Creek past Edgartown Harbor.

"David Letterman lives there. His house is part of the settlement that preserved the Herring Creek farmland from development."

"Wow," my friend replies.

One of my most vivid "real people" experiences happens on the day that Carly Simon comes to the West Tisbury School.

Carly is invited by a parent, a beautician who does her nails.

The parent is concerned about the effect of adolescent teasing on her thirteen-year-old daughter. She tells me that Carly is willing to come in and talk to the class.

"Really?" I reply with surprise. "She wants to do that?"

"Yes, she sure does," the parent affirms. "I'll be bringing her on Wednesday."

• • •

"Here she comes," secretary Sue announces.

I look out of my office window and see the beautiful performer walking toward the school, barefoot, her dog cradled in one arm and a book held in the opposite hand.

"Come into my office, Carly," I invite the singer. "Let's talk before you go to the classroom."

"Sure," she replies. She tells me that the book she holds is her diary with entries made when she was eight years old.

"I was teased too" she admits. "I understand."

I bring Carly to the sixth-grade classroom and introduce her to the students. She wants to be introduced as a parent, not as a famous person. "Carly's children went to our school," I tell the students. "She understands what it's like to be a sixth grader."

"Are you *the* Carly Simon?" one astute boy calls out.

"My name is Carly Simon," the singer replies humbly.

The boy isn't fooled. "Wait 'til I tell my mother," he exclaims.

"Will you sign my jacket?"

"After class," Carly replies.

Carly tells the students about her diary, then opens it and reads an entry from 1956. "I hate Sharon!" she begins. She tells of her humiliation and shame when she was teased as a child. The students listen attentively at first, and then the questions begin.

"Did you get angry when you were teased?"

"How did you feel?"

"Did your friends defend you?"

"Did you ever hit anybody?"

"What did your parents say?"

"Did you call names back?"

"If I tell the teacher, will they call me a tattletale?"

Carly asks that I take no pictures. She wants no recognition for the service she does this day. She signs the jacket of the boy, picks up her dog, and leaves the school as inauspiciously as she arrived.

I realize how asynchronous a Hollywood-style bus tour to spot celebrities would be here on the Vineyard. Twenty miles long, seven miles wide, the Vineyard is best traversed by foot or by bicycle and without any acclaim.

Chapter 23

HIGHWAYS AND BYWAYS

THE VINEYARD IS NOT CAR FRIENDLY, nor do the locals want it to be. The Steamship Authority is one arena in which the vehicle drama is reenacted periodically.

"Why should we make it less expensive or easier to access the Vineyard?" exasperated voices exclaim. "We don't want more people!"

"Who ever proposed a fast ferry anyway?"

No parking lots or traffic lights punctuate the Vineyard, except for the notorious yellow blinker at the intersection of the Barnes and Edgartown-Vineyard Haven Roads. The shifting of that light from a blinking red on Barnes to a blinking yellow on all four sides provokes the locals to express their views.

"I had to wait fifteen minutes," complains a Barnes Road driver.

"Well, why should we have to wait?" replies an Edgartown-Vineyard Haven driver. "There are many more of us. It's our island. Why can't they just leave things as they are?"

The locals machinate to get themselves to the ferries in time so that a standby car or truck doesn't usurp their reservation. A five-way intersection near the ferry landing mandates the consideration of one car for another. Whoever gets to the corner first goes next. Remarkably, it works.

Only when the summer tourists arrive does impatience surface and the dreaded car horn sound. At the end of my first year on the island, I, too, echo the local sentiment: "Go home. Go home to your six-lane highways and to your crowded downtowns and to your exhausting commutes. I'm happy to live where the fastest speed limit is forty-five miles per hour." I have exchanged a New Jersey commute of sixty-six miles per day on interstate highways for a long walk or a short bike ride or a six-minute drive at thirty-five miles per hour to get to work.

In October I hear a woman friend exclaim, "Fall is really here. I was driving down State Road yesterday, and two truck drivers were stopped in the middle of the road having a chat! The island is ours again."

Chapter 24

BUSINESS AS USUAL

I THINK BACK to my first year, the day I arrived solo on the island. Casting off the past seemed so easy. The first month was like an extended summer vacation. The Stonewall Pond cottage lent itself to a quiet life, and that was therapeutic after three years of being a superintendent in New Jersey. At Stonewall I briefly recaptured myself. I read, wrote, and ate fresh fish and farmer's market veggies for dinner, which conveyed the added bonus of losing fifteen pounds within a few weeks. I felt terrific. From summer into fall, my eating patterns became healthier, and, until daylight savings time, I walked each evening down Old Courthouse Road in West Tisbury and onto Dr. Fisher's ancient way. There I savored the fields, the sound of grasses challenging the wind, the lovely solitude.

By November of that first year, however, the days were darkening early, and my exercise routine was hindered by the twilight skunks that prowled the street. I tried singing in the All-Island Chorus and sampling a new yoga class, but the burdens of the job, the stress associated with the holidays, the packing, the house-hunting, and the increasingly demanding job left me exhausted. Soon I needed physical therapy for an arthritis exacerbated by my frenetic life.

I adopted Tory, a gentle eight-year-old Sheltie who could be taken in by no other family member. In addition to canine companionship, I fit dog chores into my schedule. My simple life became more complicated every day.

With Dan settled in Boston, I began spending "free" weekends flying to Philadelphia to help my daughter make preparations for her impending wedding, scheduled for July of 2002. I loved helping, but the distance and the extra trips further complicated my life.

In April, a professional conference in San Antonio that had promised to be stimulating and enjoyable was fraught instead with airline difficulties and travel delays. Forced to abandon my luggage at Logan, I caught the last Cape Air flight back to the Vineyard and arrived at the West Tisbury School just in time to deliver a short speech on the school budget at the annual town meeting. I collapsed into bed that evening and found myself unable to recover from my weariness for the next two months.

. . .

What had happened to the energy that fueled me at the start of my brave Vineyard adventure? This new life felt very much like the stress of my old, I thought. Had I brought my old world to the Vineyard with me? Had I not yet made the right changes?

Chapter 25

OLD SCRIPTS

OUR DAUGHTER'S WEDDING in Philadelphia turns out to be flawless—a Friday evening church wedding followed by a party where nearly every one of the 160 guests, from eight to eighty-five years old, dances and celebrates from 7 p.m. to midnight. I graduate to the unenviable title "mother-in-law."

Back on the Vineyard, however, the dynamics of family relationships are still marked by old scripts.

My eighty-six-year-old mother visits for a week. My mom is a gentle, soft-spoken, sweet woman, but to me, her daughter, her views reverberate loudly.

"You'll love our new home, Mom," I promise, as I open the door to the comfortable first-floor suite where she will stay. I remind her that she is welcome to come and stay as long as she wishes. She replies that she can't imagine living on the Vineyard.

"Who would want to live in a place that could only be reached by a ferry boat? What about hospitals? What will you do if you get sick?"

How dare she reject my grand plan, I think—my brave experiment, the courage that others have so admired! Suddenly I am a child again, struggling to create my own identity but still secretly wanting the blessing of my parent.

I remember years of self-doubt as, during my early adolescence, my family relocated from an urban to a suburban home, from an Italian-American haven in Medford, Massachusetts, to the WASP Lexington community of heritage and privilege and outspoken Yankee frankness. I remember my mother speaking of the parents of my new friends as "Americans." In her mind there was a clear distinction between "Italians" and "Americans." Two of my father's brothers had married "Americans"—one Swedish-American, one Irish-American. Mom loved to cook Italian delicacies for the brothers. "The Americans don't cook these things," she would say proudly, as she fed my appreciative uncles.

During my adolescence, the schizophrenia of Italian versus American troubled me. I found nothing wrong with these Americans. They spoke well, dressed well, and welcomed me warmly into their homes and lives. Unlike my mother, my father encouraged me to assimilate, to blend my urban Italian heritage into my American suburban world.

I think of the diversity of the Vineyard—of the burgeoning Portuguese-speaking Brazilian population of fishermen, landscapers, and grocery store workers, of the Native American Wampanoags with their wampum art, their cranberry and strawberry festivals, their rhythmic rituals. I wonder whether the children of these groups struggle to assimilate as I did.

On the Vineyard are families who love, families who hate, families who work, families who cannot work, families who care, families who don't, families who have insulted, families who have forgiven, families who are land-rich and income-poor, families who are income-rich and generous, families of eleven generations on the island, newcomer families, families who come from tribes and foreign fishing villages and African-American aristocracy—all these families and more live together in a hundred square miles of space.

The proximity of our neighbors tempers all we do on the Vineyard. Escape was easy in my former life. Many drove thirty miles or more from work to sleep at night, to shop for groceries, to fashion a personal world. Here there is no place to hide. A former physician on the island expressed it well when she said, "I do many of my post-surgery follow-up visits in front of the meat counter at the A&P."

. . .

Martha's Vineyard is carved with miles and miles of scenic paved bike paths.

"You can ride all day without changing gears!" a friend exclaims.

To survive here, however, I think I will need to change gears. The same old gear may work, but another may serve me a lot better.

I think of the gears in my life. *First gear* when I am tentative, when I am considering an option. *Second gear* when I am doing what is necessary to get where I have decided I must go. *Third gear* as I sail along on my designated path. *Reverse* when I decide to think again. *Neutral* when I stop as I have stopped here on this island.

I recall what I left behind when I settled here. A home. A husband. Friends. Many belongings. How little I miss my wardrobe, my jewelry, my shoes, my books, my music, and even my memorabilia. Can I clear my life of more? I wonder. What will I dispense with now?

Chapter 26

TIME WARP

"A TIME WARP! LIVING IN THIS PLACE is like living in a time warp," a frustrated islander complains to a confidante at the local market. "It's the nineteen-fifties everywhere! Can't they modernize? These folks are tied to their past!"

Why do people hold on so tightly to their pasts? I wonder. I certainly experience that at the West Tisbury School. The students at this school are the best I've known anywhere—eager, energetic, easy to manage. For the kids, the school is a wonderful place to learn. However, the attitudes of a few staff members surprise me.

Dynamic teaching, creative technology, and state-of-the-art reading and writing and math strategies butt against the intransigence of those who yearn for the days when eight teachers staffed the school, the days before frameworks and standards, declining enrollment and shrinking revenues, the days when principals had fewer financial and political responsibilities. I am a force of change at the school, appreciated by some but not by others.

School dramas intensify. I am caught in a vise—on one side squeezed by distraught taxpayers who eye per-pupil costs with suspicion and mistrust, on the other side squeezed by those who want the school to operate as it has in the past, regardless of finances. Beset by growing fiscal woes and drastic reductions in state revenue, for example, I am asked to "find" $500,000 to reduce the school's budget just two weeks before school opens.

In addition to the financial dramas, political and interpersonal dramas continue, especially in wintertime when there are few diversions on the island.

"Don't worry," some console me. "It's not you; it's an island thing."

But I do worry. I tire of the effort needed to maintain harmony at the school, of the e-mail wars, and of the human and organizational frailties. I realize that I have the capability and the work ethic to do this job, but I have lost the desire. For years, adrenalin fueled me as I faced problem-solving situations—I enjoyed the challenge and the excitement. I realize that I'm not enjoying these challenges any more. If my dad were alive, he'd undoubtedly smile and say what he always did. "The first hundred years are the hardest, Elaine."

But I don't have a hundred years. Instead, I have an opportunity, still largely untapped, to slow down my life and to do what is meaningful rather than what is required.

I am offered an extended contract to continue my service to the school. I think of the teachers who have asked me to stay and of those who will celebrate when I leave. For six months, I consider the value of my energy and efforts in this school setting. I think of all the wonderful teachers and other school staff but realize that they will continue to be terrific with or without me. I remember the words of a confidante: "Will you save your life or savor it?" Should I save my job or savor my life? I ask myself.

I've considered this question before, when I left New Jersey. Suddenly I know the answer. I know what I must give up next, just as I gave up the old home and the trappings of my past when I came here. It's time to give up the work regimen I have followed since I was fourteen years old.

I complete my commitment to my original three-year contract but decide to give myself the gift of enjoying the Vineyard without a consuming sixty-hour-per-week job. I am old enough to realize that I am not indispensable. I resign with no regrets and turn over the principalship to an eager successor. I miss the people at the school, especially the children and the good friends, but I don't miss the job.

I accept the inevitability of change. I remember that the Vineyard once was barren of trees and home to more than ten thousand sheep.

Its protected waters were a major waterway for vessels sailing from Europe to New York and Philadelphia. In 500 years, with the current rate of coastal erosion, the Vineyard may be no more.

As for me, I've grown to love the old-fashioned, unassuming nature of the place, and I'm happy to be able to accept it without the obligation to change anything. I don't cease to be delighted by the humble wooded paths that lead to amazing vistas. Tucked away are the ancient ways, the original carriage trails that remind us that history is important. As I walk along one of these ancient ways now, I meet a beetlebung with its beckoning arms.

Beetlebung Tree

A bevy of rabbits darts into the bushes. A gaggle of wild turkeys crosses my path. A red-tailed falcon flies overhead. Like meandering on ancient trails, we often abandon the paved roadways to find the treasures. I ground myself to the earth as my Vineyard yoga classes have taught me to do, and I celebrate my walk and my self with deep Kripalu breaths.

Chapter 27

FELLOW TRAVELER

THE FERRY *ISLANDER* snakes around the Falmouth lighthouse as it approaches the Woods Hole terminal. It is February 2005, four years after I began my Vineyard adventure. I gaze out the time-worn ferry windows—windows that have fogged from the warm breath of cold noses; windows that have welcomed the finger tracings of small children. On the port side, I see harbor seals, their blubber draped across the icy rocks.

I remember the cormorants I saw in Falmouth on that August day when I first arrived-hopeful, eager, energetic, searching.

Dan sits beside me. He has been my fellow traveler for thirty-seven years. Bewildered at first, he later accepted my Vineyard adventure without anger or recrimination.

Though he'd never make such a choice, Dan knows me well enough to honor mine. Four different divorcees remark, "If I had that kind of partner, I'd still be married today!"

After three years working in Cambridge and commuting to the Vineyard every weekend, Dan decides to retire and to join me full time. We relearn the art of living together daily—waking, sleeping, cooking, exercising, socializing, paying bills, relegating space and time.

For most of our adult lives we awoke to an alarm clock and went to sleep, not when we were tired, but whenever the meetings and schedules and other obligations ended. Some nights we didn't sleep at all. We sleep now.

We revel in our fortune to have landed in such a breath-taking place. Sand vehicles steer us past Mytoi and to the hidden coves of Cape Pogue in Chappaquiddick. Ospreys and eagles soar above us at Felix Neck. Stone remnants of deserted villages tease our imaginations at Middle Road Sanctuary. Kayaks lead us to the recesses of Stonewall Pond and under the roadway to where the tides are stronger. We walk westward around the Nat's Farm meadow as the sun sets. At Lambert's Cove, the pond on the left at the crest of the hill is a cobalt surprise before the path tilts to the right and opens to the sound. Ours are the first snowshoe tracks in the state forest near our home after a winter snow.

Our favorite spot is the winter entrance to Long Point, at the end of three dirt miles on Deep Bottom Road. There we cut through a short wooded trail to the green-gray grasses that stretch along the dunes between Long and Great Ponds. We wonder if this same stretch once hosted the wood vines and gooseberries and raspices and eglantine described by Gosnold upon his arrival in 1602. We hike the Long Point trail to the ocean again and again, but we still stop to catch our breath every time the grassy fields and the dunes and the ponds and the ocean unfold in front of us.

"Happy?" Dan asks me.

"Yup," I reply.

I Am Already

One flow of
energy and breath
connects the full
depth and breadth
of consciousness.

There is nowhere to
go but here, no time
but now, no why or
how or maybe—just
the knowing, simple and complete, that I
am already what I
thought I had to seek.

from *One Soul: More Poems from the Heart of Yoga* by Danna Faulds, Peaceable Kingdom Books, Greenville, Virginia

A discussion guide and additional copies of this memoir are available from the author:

Elaine Pace

P.O. Box 1346

West Tisbury, Massachusetts 02575

epace614@adelphia.net

www.memories101.us

www.ingramcontent.com/pod-product-compliance
Lightning Source LLC
LaVergne TN
LVHW091007080826
845145LV00003B/1165

9781595409478